Morphing in
STILLNESS

A STORY OF LOVE, LOSS AND THE BEAUTY OF TRANSFORMATION

LUZ ARTEAGA-PRAY

© Luz Arteaga-Pray

Cover design:Gloria Arteaga
Copy editor: Melanie Gendreau

ISBN: 978-1-66780-742-3

DEDICATION

This book is dedicated to all my "Warrior Sisters & Brothers" who in choosing to be vulnerable in my presence through sharing their messy, scary and beautiful experiences, allowed me to step into my own courageous wisdom. Thank you to all the authors, speakers, and truth tellers I quote in this book and the many more like:

Oprah Winfrey

Pema Chodron

Esther Hicks

Diane Ackerman

TABLE OF CONTENTS

IN THE BEGINNING

The vibe of the summer of 1990 was very different on Thayer Street in Providence, Rhode Island. Thayer Street was alive all year round due to its proximity to Brown University and Rhode Island School of Design. However, there was always an abrupt changing of the guards, so to speak, in the summer – as it became a popular hangout destination for local teens. That was the summer my whole life changed.

After graduating high school I went straight to cosmetology school. I landed a job as an assistant to the head stylist at an upscale salon just steps from the infamous street. My boss had a big clientele, and in order to accommodate them all, he would work very long hours, which meant I had to work very long hours. I didn't mind, though. All my friends were at college, and I wanted to focus on building a career. Being so focused, I didn't have much time for partying or socializing. To be honest, I liked that I didn't have any distractions. I was really determined to watch, learn, and take in everything my mentor was willing to pass on to me about the industry. He was gifted, sophisticated, and his clients thought he walked on water. So that was the person I wanted to learn from. One of the reasons that the trendy street had an interesting energy that summer was because the Brown Bookstore, across the street from the salon, hired a construction company to put an addition on the store. They needed to finish the project before students got back in September, so the construction crew was very big.

The first time I saw him, I thought how physically perfect God had made this person. There were about thirty construction workers in a small space, but he stood out to me. Apparently, he stood out to a bunch of other people. I had clients come in and say, "Did you see the guy across the street?!" Not once or twice, but a bunch of times. I would always respond, "Which one? There are thirty guys over there!" but I knew the buzz was about him. He had dark hair, tan skin, and his skin looked so soft because it shined in the light. Maybe he was a mix of cultures, Italian? Greek? Portuguese? I was not sure, but . . . Wow!

That summer I was working five days a week, twelve-hour days, and because the project at the bookstore needed to be done by the time students got back, he had the same schedule I did. By this time, we could not help but notice each other. Being an apprentice, you also became everyone's "gofer." So, I was sent on a lot of errands during the day, which allowed me to catch a glimpse of the hot construction worker everyone was talking about. I would pass by so much that I started to know the rest of the crew at the site – not him though. We would greet each other, but that was it. He seemed shy and reserved, and that, was so hot.

One day at the salon, I came across a name on my schedule that I didn't recognize. That was normal since I had just started to build my clientele. Well, what do you know? John was his name, and with a dirty tank top, ripped jeans, and filthy work boots, he sat patiently in our very elegant and modern waiting area until someone, who was to become his hairstylist, called his name. The thoughts that circulated in my mind were of pure judgment. "He's too beautiful to be nice!" I thought. "He must be a total dickhead!" Boy was I wrong. He was soft-spoken, kind, personable, and came across very genuine. Hay Dios mio!

Our conversation came naturally since we were now familiar with each other because of all the errands I would do during the day for my boss. The haircut felt like our first date. We asked each other all the questions one does on a first date. So, where are you from? Where did you go to school? How are you so beautiful? Uugh... I asked myself that ... in my head ... you know ... not out loud. I pride myself in being a very precise and accurate men's haircutter. I was booked every half hour, and my boss was very impressed with my efficient work and timing. However, when I cut John's hair, it took an hour and a half.

That summer, all of Thayer Street kept a close eye on us – my colleagues, the employees of the convenience store we would often go to, even workers at some of the restaurants we would have lunch at sometimes because our long days did not allow for proper dates. So, we stole a half hour here and there to get to know each other. It was really sweet, comfortable and natural.

Our courtship was very special. Our work ethics, beliefs, family values, and overall outlook on life seemed to line up to who we, together, became. We dated for five years. John became a regular part of my family very quickly. He would offer himself for projects with my brothers. He was thoughtful in that, at times, he would send me roses at the salon "just because." I was never one for flowers, but from him, I was more than happy to receive them. He would sometimes take the time to write in the cards that came with the flowers, little love messages in Spanish to impress me. He always impressed me.

It didn't take much to impress me when it came to him. I was never the girl who dreamed of Prince Charming nor the kind of wedding I would have or the dress I would wear. I never knocked those beliefs or desires – they just weren't mine.

TWO WORLDS
COLLIDE

grew up in a family of eight children. We came from Medellin, Colombia to the United States to reunite with our dad and two older brothers. Our dad was determined to educate us in the States, so he and my brothers came before the rest of us to find the right community for us to settle. There was a town where many Colombian families were migrating to, but Cumberland, Rhode Island was where our dad chose to plant *our* roots and *completely* surround us in an all English-speaking community. We landed in a town of Portuguese and white Americans. Our dad also saw the opportunities available at Cumberland High School being a Division 1 school. Since three of my brothers excelled in soccer, dad knew they would be in a perfect position to thrive.

After my father's death four years after our arrival, we were forced into assisted living. My mom was going to college and there were six of us still in school. The first few years after my dad's death were very difficult, but we all knew we needed to pull our own weight in the household and get jobs to make ends meet. I was still too young to work. Watching my mom and older siblings' efforts to find a place in this new culture, I was shown that making a living, surviving, and being relevant in society was to be my purpose. Marriage was not in my plans, and a prince, a wedding, and a dress, were just not my priority.

John came from a family of five generations of farmers, Portuguese and English, a direct descendent of Roger Williams, as a matter of fact. They were simple, loving, hard-working people. So hard-working that as soon as you learned how to walk, picking corn was the first game you learned how to play. I admired the commitment to the family business. There was much pride in continuing the tradition.

John eventually became a civil engineer. I also admired that he walked his own path while clearly carrying the pride of where he came from. It oozed from him in everything he did and how he chose to live his life. Although we were raised very differently, John and I seemed to complement each other. I believe what really pulled us together, besides how physically attracted we were to each other, was the fact that sports played a big role in our lives. I not only danced in a program for gifted and talented students in my high school (one of only two high schools in the state that had this program), I also played basketball and softball for my high school. On the weekends, after my own lessons, I taught ice skating to little kids. Oh yeah – I also played soccer for my brothers at our local Boys & Girls Club.

John, too, was very athletic. He played football and baseball for his high school and excelled in both, farm chores allowing. Being so active and not having gone to college right away, we had to find opportunities to keep sports in our lives. I managed to continue to play softball in a summer league. When John and I were seriously dating, he actually became my coach. I loved it! So did the other ladies on the team. In the meantime, John managed to stay active as well. After high school, he was able to play semi-pro football. Unfortunately, he got hurt and did not return. He joined a co-ed softball league and assisted in coaching a high school freshman baseball team. We ultimately, a little later, were a part of a co-ed volleyball team in our town. Sports was the glue we could count on.

June 11, 1995, was our wedding day. The day was cool and drizzly, but we didn't care. We felt so blessed to have each other. Our families, though very different, loved each other too. We were truly blessed with this union. The wedding took place outdoors on the family farm under a tent. The unpredictable weather brought out John's family's creative mode. So many special elements contributed to the overall country ambiance: from the flower baskets floating on the pond; to the newly built gazebo decorated in farm-grown wildflowers – where our ceremony took place; to the sweet, artisan scent of sawdust on the ground under the tent – which absorbed the moisture from the drizzly day. There were even small trees tied to the main poles inside the tent to make it look like they grew inside. His family did not miss a beat.

My family and I had a few tricks up our sleeves too. The first one being that I arrived on a horse and carriage. The clippity-clop of the horse's hooves on the road to where I was to marry the man of my dreams gave everyone chills. The music did not start on time, of course, but even that was perfect, because all you could hear was the horse coming down the road. My father passed away when I was ten, so I asked my brothers to walk me down the aisle. As the carriage approached the place where I would begin my journey to the alter, my brothers got in their positions along the stone walkway. One by one, they handed me over to the next brother, five brothers in total. The tiny moments I had with each brother, whether it was a stare we shared or words of well wishes for their little sister, the act of them passing me on all the way to my mom, then ultimately to John, is so difficult to put into words.

Being the baby of the family, with my siblings anyway, I believe these momentous experiences tend to hit a little harder. When I tell you that our love inspired some miracles that day that is an understatement. One was, John's brother in-law, who had not spoken to his wife's family (John's sister) for ten years, felt so inspired by the event that from that day on, he put his issues aside and began a relationship with my in-laws. My two-year-old niece, who had not yet started to walk, chose that day to take her first steps. Oh yes, I cannot forget how the sun beautifully broke through the clouds.

I think the best surprise was when my voice came through the speakers, John recognizing it was me singing a love song for him — but my mouth wasn't moving. I couldn't do it live because I knew I would burst into tears; so I went to a recording studio and had the song professionally recorded. John cried like a little girl. So did everyone present that day witnessing our union. It was really special as cars passing by would stop to watch the country wedding. When we were announced man and wife, what we thought were fireworks in the distance, went off at the perfect time. Later, we found out it was a gun at the gun club nearby.

Our first five years of marriage were great. We each lived with our parents up until our wedding. We had plans of building a home on the land we had bought that abutted the family farm. In the meantime, we invested in an RV. It was the very first thing we owned as a couple. Although it was a 1972 tin box, we felt like grown-ups, together for the first time. It was so small that turning on a candle heated the whole place. There were also times that were a bit challenging, like when microwaving a potato and having the TV on would cause the power to go out. Also, we only had access to one channel. We felt like we were thrust into the future when we were able to see how many channels Direct TV had.

We ended up living on the land in the RV for five years. After his long day at work, John would come home to clear more land. He did most of the structural work himself to save money. You could even find me once in a while, at seven months pregnant, on a ladder painting the border outside the house. (Please do not tell my mom.)

WHEN THE
FUN BEGINS

F ive years into our marriage and a beautiful little baby girl later, we were in our home, the home that required blood, sweat, and tears and took so long to build. That's right, the day we came home from the hospital with our newborn was the day John was able to get our occupancy permit. He was working so hard to get all the town red tape processes done so we could legitimately be in our home. John's boss at the time, who didn't really know how down to the wire we were, gave John a hard time about leaving early that day knowing his wife and baby were coming home. John finally broke and gracefully quit. Yup, a huge home, a new baby, and my husband quit his job. That was terrifying at the time, but in hindsight – so worth it. I would do it all over again. I was actually very impressed and proud, and later really weepy because of those damn hormones.

Our marriage was full of adventures, love and family. Our daughter was the sweetest, cutest, easygoing toddler. She was a girly girl and no doubt a daddy's girl. I grew up hanging out with my brothers who were close to me in age. I don't know if that was the reason, but I was no girly girl. Soon after our daughter turned two, our son was born. I will just say he was very different from his sister. My daughter wanted to include the world in all her experiences, while my son wanted a background check on anyone coming within eight feet of him! I would come to use the word "intense" for him – a lot. When he was three, our third child was born – a boy. I don't know that he ever really cried – I mean, like, ever. I swear, this one woke up every morning singing. He smiled all the time. The dynamic was above and beyond what we could have imagined. Three happy, healthy, easygoing kids. You just can't mess with that. Right? Or could we? Deep down, I felt unsettled. Dare we mess with perfection and go for one more down the road? We were in the momentum of getting the hang of family and how to navigate it all. Yet, as time went on, I did not feel complete. Nevertheless, John convinced me we should not mess with what he considered a great situation.

We made it clear. We were done. We were a family of five. So, I took it upon myself to make sure our decision was final. I asked John, as the patriarch of our family and my life partner, to take one for the team so we would not have to worry about getting pregnant again. He didn't seem comfortable with the idea, then again, most men are not comfortable with it. I handed him some information I had gotten from my doctor for him to read at his pace. He had read the pamphlets and taken in the information. I assured him it was a common procedure and an easy recovery. In time, I reminded him I would make the appointment for him. I would gently approach him seeing he was uneasy with the idea. I figured "when he is ready." I know he sympathized with me having had three C-sections. It just made sense he would take this one for us — for me. I believe this is where our disconnect became a thing for me.

TO MY SURPRISE

On December 18, 2007, baby number four came into our lives. Absolute perfection. Another boy. Now we had a tribe to help and love our new little bundle of joy. This one definitely walked to the beat of his own drum. Literally. This kid woke up dancing in the morning. I thought, "Oh good! I'll finally have my dancer." (Not only did I dance when I was younger, I also did some singing.) He was musical and could care less about kicking a ball around. His siblings were very athletic, like their mom, but more like dad.

To my surprise, I very much enjoyed motherhood. I felt blessed to be chosen to be the mom of four of the coolest people I've ever come to know. You can just imagine how busy we were. In addition to working full time, John coached the kids in whatever sport they were doing at the time – what a gift. Not only that, John was an awesome coach. I often expressed that I thought he should have done it professionally. He had a gift for getting the kids to listen and a keen sense for getting his players to their own next level. And oh yes, the parents. John had some mad skills in the way he spoke to the parents about their children. That was always interesting to me because John was not much of a talker, yet when it came to the kids, sports, and the parents, he was very clear in getting his thoughts across.

Those years were magical and at the same time challenging. In 2005, I owned my own salon. John took on most of the household duties including play dates, birthday parties and pool parties. He seemed to have a community behind him, though. When your children do sports, the community becomes your social circle, so John had a lot of support. It is fair to say the business consumed a lot of me. I believe it took a big toll on our relationship. There were times I would stay at work, knowing I would be late and I didn't want to mess with the dynamic of what he had going on – the kids, the popular coach, and the support of all those families. I became an outsider. Looking back now, I made myself an outsider. I felt separate from the life my family, at that time, was living. I can truly say, I began to feel I had no place where they were. John was juggling all the balls and the kids were thriving. What was my purpose?

In 2014, my salon flooded which was actually a blessing in disguise. I decided not to re-open as the responsibilities of running my own salon and raising a family were overwhelming. My good friends, Yvonne and Billy, owned a salon up the street and they let me rent a chair there. This was my opportunity to contribute to my family everyday. I was thrilled not to have the pressure of running a business and looked forward to reconnecting with my home life, especially with my husband. The chance to be a couple again inside our family unit gave me great joy – until we settled into the day-to-day reality.

John ran his home like clockwork. I seemed to be in his way. We knew it would take some time to get used to me being home more. It wasn't pretty, but I managed to find my domestic feet again. I became consumed by how we could be a couple again. I felt I had to make up for so much lost time. Funny, I never thought we had to make up for lost time – maybe because I always felt it was all on me. I don't know why. Maybe because his role was so established in our family? I guess having a business while the children were so active and young, made me feel like I did not contribute to day-to-day family life. Or was it that I was made to believe I had a lot of catching up to do? Either way, I was struggling to connect with my husband.

I came to understand our idea of family time was very different. I would make plans with the six of us and he would add a family or two. That's fair, I thought, we were spending time with our family and other families. On the rare occasion we had an opportunity for a date night, John would add one or two other couples. Once again, I thought, okay it's not the time together I thought we spoke of, but okay. The evening would always end up with the husbands in one room talking about sports and the wives in another room drinking wine and sharing recipes.

There were times I would pack up the car and take the kids to the beach, or go exploring, or just go on some random adventure. John would always take that opportunity to work in the yard. Although disappointed, I understood. The work was therapeutic, and he took a lot of pride in the yard work. When he wasn't working, he was coaching. If he wasn't coaching, he was working in the yard. There were times he would be invited to play in golf tournaments during the week. I always thought, "Oh good, he is treating himself to do something he loves." In small corners of my mind, I was disappointed that when I would ask him to play hooky with me for the day, it was never a good day to do that. Okay, that is how all marriages are, right? All I wanted was to be a couple in the small nooks of our busy lives, even catching up in bed talking about what was new or connecting on stupid stuff. To feel like we were on the same team. Still aiming for the same things and if not, to discover why we weren't.

DIFFERENT
PLAINS

After a while, "working in the yard" got old. We had friends with the same number of kids, at the same point in life. I would always hear what they did on the nights they were alone. I would hear about the family trips they took. I simply wanted my husband to myself once in a while. Was that too much to ask?

I always spoke of bringing the family to visit relatives in Colombia, where I am from. I looked forward to someday showing them where I came from and what they, through me, were a part of. I made plans three times for a trip there. Three times he never took seriously or thought it was real. He never made the attempt to acknowledge we had a trip coming up – and so, no trip ever happened.

What am I doing wrong? Why couldn't I inspire my husband to want to know all of me? What am I missing? Our neighbor, married to a woman from Venezuela, had been there a bunch of times. What was I not getting? It's me. I need to self-evaluate. I need to go within. I need to work on myself and feel good about me. Then he will reflect back how I feel about myself. Right?

I read new books. I found new interests. I committed to my health and wellness. I would make sure I complimented his fathering skills in front of the children and how impressed we always were of him so he would feel like our king. I enhanced my life experience, unfortunately, John never reflected it back.

When did this disconnect happen? John would tell me, later on, everything he did was for me. Then how did it come across as neglect? How did my efforts do the same? It was a constant going up to bat, swinging and missing – every time. There were moments of light, but we were never able to maintain it.

I became emotionally starved and drained. We chose to mask our issues. We never for one minute though thought about calling it quits. We did couples therapy and learned so much about ourselves and each other. It was just too late for me. Every day our disconnect chiseled away at my spirit. If the man I believed was perfect, even in his flaws, does not understand the languages I attempted to speak in order to keep this union intact, what does one do? How long does one continue this very uncoordinated dance?

I came to the conclusion nothing was wrong with John. He dealt the only way he knew how, all while going through his own pain. There was nothing wrong with me either. I tried to communicate what I needed and gave myself the attention I thought I was lacking, which is what I knew to do. We simply no longer understood each other. We lived on separate plains. Our dreams of us, would have eventually led us in different directions. Don't get me wrong, I believe we could be compatible with a lot of people, but I felt so unheard for so long that it was just too late for me with us. I want to be clear, when it came to my life with my children, I stood strong and there was no doubt of who I was, what I gave, and what came back from our bond. However, with John and I, we did not prioritize each other in the way we both felt loved. Was I really considering putting an end to this journey with this beautiful being? The life we built was beautiful, four great kids, a big house. What will our families say? Where will I go?

If I wanted to be emotionally and mentally healthy again, I needed to say goodbye to this adventure. Come to peace that this wonderful journey, overall, had come to an end, for me. The struggle was how I was going to express to this man I respected so much that this was not a rejection of him, but a becoming of me. When getting quiet enough to come to that truth, my heart began to heal and a peace came over my body. Comprehending that some people are meant to pass through our journey teaching and showing us and contributing to the whole of who we are is just part of the human experience. I feel grateful that John was a precious gift in my life – then and still. The union I had come to know and love had outgrown me or I it. Recognizing the alchemy that was happening in front of me was in and of itself the beauty of a new form of me. This is when my transformation began.

The summer of 2018 I finally, again, bought tickets to visit family in Colombia. It was an opportunity to be in this difficult process while being a family still. I believe John thought this was a window of maybe coming closer. I believed it was an opportunity to prove we, John and I, could put our issues aside and be a family in difficult times. The trip was magical. The kids surprised themselves in that they did not need me to translate all the time. They were able to communicate in day-to-day conversation. I was so proud and they were too! We experienced Colombia as a family, and it really set the tone to go forward separating in love.

The goal was peace, as long as I came from a place of truth, compassion, and love, the rest was up to him. His response or reaction was on him. I had to hang onto what I knew for myself. Being the wise man John is, we agreed to separate in grace and inside of love. Since peace was the goal and since the house was on family land, I chose not to fight for it or for half of his inheritance. The kids were most important in this process. The house had always been the children's home. We didn't want the kids to bounce back and forth between homes. I was able to find a studio two minutes away in our town. John even inspected it for me, making sure it was safe and close by.

It was really important that the kids see we could do difficult things, still inside of love and respect. They needed to see that we loved each other, just not like a husband and wife. They needed to see that although our structure as a family looked different, we were family till the end, especially, John and me. This is when we let them in on our decision to divorce. Their response was exactly how you'd imagine young kids who idolize their parents would respond. We broke their hearts. No matter how much we explained how John and I respected and loved each other, and were family till the end, *we broke their hearts.* We still stayed strong in their mental absorption of the news. We went on faith that they would be fine. And if not, it was our job to take the hit – no matter how it manifested. We were determined, in the discomfort of this process, to be a safe place for the kids to feel the good, the bad, and the ugly.

THE DANGER OF PERCEPTION

My disconnect from our partnership was a ten-year process of going back and forth. What is wrong with me? I have to be the one to keep this intact. I have to fix me. I am not a good wife. All these thoughts made me feel what I refer to as "uncoupleable." I felt so guilty and responsible about creating so much hurt that there was no way I could be, or work toward, being part of a couple. I really needed to work on myself. Explore how "I" got here.

My inability to find a way for John to see me and understand the impact of our disconnect left me feeling irrelevant. I think it is important to point out that John and I not only loved each other in our dysfunction, we really liked each other. I was never uncomfortable in his presence nor did I dread coming home. In our family life, with our kids in sports and everything surrounding the children, we still did very well. Our arguments were never heated, it just wasn't our style. We were able to put our stuff as a couple aside, but also used our family life as an excuse not to deal with us.

Ending a thirty-year union weighed heavily on me. There was the guilt of knowing I broke the heart of a person I loved and respected and the possibility of messing up my kids. What scenario did I not think of? And yet, having a thirty-year relationship that produced four of the coolest people I have ever come to know was in no way a failure in my eyes. Nevertheless, I leaned into this uncomfortable place of transmutation. I got off social media. I didn't go out or socialize and I turned up the volume on my meditations and got as quiet and as still as I could. I needed to listen and really hear what my inner voice was trying to say. I was very focused on blocking off any noise that would interfere with my process of cleansing my thoughts. Staying true to myself was instrumental in order to stay in a strong, loving place for everyone involved. I learned to notice anything that showed up in my meditations and simply let it be. Whatever was popping up, I was determined to look at it, observe it, and allow it to move me to my next right place in myself. So there I was, in my new apartment, trying to take steps forward. I was creating experiences he never wanted to have with me; nutruing my rich friendships; engaging in stimulating conversations and starting my evolution. I felt free, not from John, but from the thoughts and beliefs that no longer served me.

UNCHARTERED TERRITORY

n March 2020 the world shut down. The first two weeks were fun. Lots of Netflix, at home catching up on shows I was told about and never had the time to watch. I wasn't allowed to work. Fun, right? We later find out there was a global pandemic called Coronavirus, aka COVID-19. We all were forced to SIT . . . GO NOWHERE . . . HAVE NO CONTACT . . . NO GOING OUTSIDE OF OUR OWN HOMES . . . JUST GREAT!

I lived alone for the first time in my life. I was going to travel, create new experiences, and explore my new reality. The universe had other plans for me. It said to me, "Not so fast Luz, this time is here for you. Use it to guide you. Use this time to love yourself. Use this time as a springboard to evolve. It will not be easy, but I promise, it will be worth it." Really?!

This time in quarantine actually brought peaceful moments I really loved. Three weeks in, and I cannot even tell you how many bottles of wine later (don't judge), I began the work. The inner work. The work that requires a painful honesty. The work that I had read about. The personal work that required me to look at my participation in the breakdown of my marriage. The work that recognized the warped perception that eventually caused me to be so disconnected in my partnership and inside the institution of my marriage. Most importantly recognizing the misalignment with myself that contributed to the ending of the life I knew.

The work consisted of making a regular schedule of meditating. It would entail going to bed with a particular thought, and without judging it or trying to fix it, going to sleep. In the morning, that would be the thought I would meditate on. For example, at bedtime, I would ask myself "Could I have communicated differently on how serious I thought our dysfunction was?" Then going to sleep and allowing the statement to simply exist, without trying to fix or judge it. Just letting it be. As we sleep, we let go of any resistance because we are resting. It is the perfect state of mind for meditating. So, my mornings consisted of being with that statement and listening to what answers would transpire.

I came to understand that the answers that came to me were always in the form of some kind of forgiveness. I needed to forgive myself for reacting to situations that triggered real emotions for me. Forgiving myself for thinking John owed me my joy in life. Forgiving John for being himself and responding the only way he knew how . . . in silence and distance.

The three months out of the labor force, not knowing what this airborne monster was going to morph into and the uncertainty of how to live our lives from here on in, became the most beautiful time I had ever experienced. Being forced to sit in silence brought up not only all my insecurities that were a contributing factor to the end of my relationship with my husband, but also a new way to see the relationship with myself.

I began to see myself as a person who just got back from war. I discovered the war was with myself though. Having the courage to go so deep within and seeing the flawed being that I am, inspired the ugly cry. At the same time, there was a relief in knowing I just got through a very difficult step in my evolution. I felt I had conquered a disconnection with my being. This was really good stuff. This was when I began a fitness regimen and also an all plant-based lifestyle. I was cleansing my mind so I continued the work with my body. I believe that my saving grace in quarantine were my kids, whom I saw every day since they were only two minutes away from my studio. They were the only people I saw face-to-face. I think this was the best part of this time for me.

This chaotic time also gave me an opportunity to dive into all the books I use in my life for constant guidance and understanding. I have a collection of personal growth books from mentors that I often rotate according to what is happening in my life. One quote that helped me through this time is from the book *When Things Fall Apart* by Pema Chodron. "The most fundamental aggression and harm to ourselves, is to remain ignorant by not having the courage and respect to look at ourselves honestly and gently."

Other insightful reads that moved me are *The Teachings of Abraham* and *The Astonishing Power of Emotions*, by Esther and Jerry Hicks. An excerpt that stood out to me is "Let your feelings be your guide, your emotions are your indicators." Of course, I don't know what my life would be like if I did not have this visionary in my life: Ms. Oprah Winfrey. I had the privilege to see her and other great speakers in Baltimore, Maryland for a whole weekend with my sisters, Estella and Gloria. This was one of the highlights of my life. One of Oprah's most impactful statements that has always resonated with me is "Think like a queen, a queen is not afraid to fail. She knows failure is another stepping-stone to greatness."

FOG BEGINS
TO LIFT

believe that what is meant for us will simply present itself. I believe my true friends, which are the family I chose, will continue to love, support, and respect me, unconditionally. I believe that the awakening happening at this moment in time, especially for us dreamers, seekers, artists, and lovers of life, is most fruitful in the quiet nooks of moments. For it is in those moments that we know for sure how precious life is, no matter what's happening. That in that moment, it is bliss. I believe that there are gifts to be found looking to our past in the way of reflection, but we must never live there – for you will block what is meant for you. (I think Oprah said that one.) I also believe some pain is worth hanging onto. There are wounds that never really heal. We simply learn to live with them. The fact is, although faint, the scars are here to stay. There are also old wounds we make space for inside us, to remind us of the pain that ultimately becomes *the gift* we could not have possibly seen the moment it was created. Some pain is meant to stay simply to teach us we are able to survive yet again. It is also worth hanging onto some pain to remind us in times of doubt and despair, that we are alive.

When we experience a level of joy, we are in complete alignment with who we really are. When that isn't happening, it is our obligation to discover and unwrap it and find out why. It is our birthright to be in and move through this world in joy. Joy is an indication of being closer to the beings we came in as. Think about it. Babies are pure love. No one teaches them that. They just are. If we aim to get back to that state, we can return to the person we were meant to be – before we got sidetracked by the all the noise and distractions in our life. We will become the essence, the force, the light, and the love we truly are. Coming to the realization of my circumstance made me feel aligned with myself for the first time in a very long time.

It was only in quiet and willingness to look inside without judgment that I was able to embrace all of me. Even if it meant ending my marriage. I have a long way to go when it comes to the new way of looking at the relationship with the father of my children. I understand that our biggest problem we have in common is our humanness, which is also what made this union and separation so beautiful and so painful.

The moral of my story is this: there is no blame here. It is no one's fault (and all our fault) that our marriage ended. This was simply the natural progression of my life. Natural progression shows up in all sorts of ways no matter how good or bad your life seems, the circumstances you encounter – or even who we have as president. (I could not help that one.) Point being, there is no one way to live a life. If only we were taught that from the time we were born. We are born with our very own GPS that never breaks, never steers us in the wrong direction. We just need to trust that our inner navigation leads us on the path we were each uniquely gifted.

BECOMING

Ultimately, we are the force that needs to look within and determine who we are. We must be willing to get quiet enough to hear our own truth, as hard as it is to hear. We must be willing to get still enough in order for our awakening to begin. Still enough to feel our way to our next right place. So quiet, that without effort, we are able to morph in the stillness and space of our destined evolvement. One way or another these moments show up in our lives, and our obligation is to listen. We need to open our minds and hearts to what life is trying to give and show us.

Maybe I would have allowed myself to listen to my inner voice when my circumstances "felt" not right instead of being so conditioned to do what our society says we're supposed to do. "Stick it out," society says. Just the word "stick" sounds, to me, like "suck it up buttercup," "tolerate," "put up with," "till death do us part." You get the picture. This kind of language does not leave any room for two uniquely flawed people to evolve. As I've come to learn, unity within a couple only works when each person is aligned with who they are as individuals. In order to grow as a couple, each partner must understand, support and respect the other's personal growth. That is the work. Choosing one another again and again throughout that process is the gift.

I have come to know that whatever life presents to me, whether good or bad, ultimately is for my greater good. It is life guiding me to level up. I have faith that it is always a gift. A gift for me and only me, to be used so I can continue the journey of my becoming, and that is my gift to the world. I still have moments of emotional throwing up, but not at John, and that is progress. The truth is it has only been a year. I must live in a space of being proud of how far I have come through this. When I begin to be hard on myself, I remind myself that our kids are not only doing well, but they continue to thrive on every level. John and I did that. The ending of this beautiful union I hold so dear, that produced four amazing people, is in no way a failure. It is an embedded fiber that has transformed the foundation for the next chapter in my life. I hope to pass this language on to my children so they will learn the worthiness of listening to and honoring their emotions through the evolution of their own lives.

According to Esther Hicks in *The Teachings of Abraham*, "We are not the creators of a painting or a sculpture or a book. We are creators of the moment of the flow. The 'art' is the translation of a perfect moment. Finding the moment of connection with ourselves will always create a flow, a movement that lines up with who we truly are. You are not the creator of a painting. You are the creator of the 'moment' "of 'being' a painter." We create our own realities. However, it is only through our awareness of each step of the journey that we can truly become who we are meant to be. It is in the process of one's journey that one becomes, not in the accomplishment or destination itself.

My purpose for sharing my story through this medium is to explore my part in the dismantling and slow crumble of my marriage and why I came to the decision to end it with a good man, knowing many women who would do anything to meet one. I have come to understand that in "becoming" comes a process of "unbecoming." An awareness of unlearning all that was taught to us from our parents and surroundings growing up. For me, it meant being taught to see men as the decision makers. If a man is providing a home for you to live in, and works really hard, that is a noble quality to have in a partner and should be enough to make you happy. Unlearning the conventional roles that I saw growing up never sat well with me. I thought it just had to be that way. So where does one begin? Who do I look to? Who thinks this way?

I was going to have to be brave enough to find my own way at the cost of my marriage. Go against everything I was taught about how to be in this world and examine what I saw of how couples existed in a partnership. Starting with simply being a girl. You know, the basics – being told to wear pretty dresses, play with dolls, and stay pristine. I was already off to a very bad start. I was taught to be soft and pretty (like I had any control over that.) I felt pretty lucky though, by the time I was born, my siblings had more influence in raising me than my parents did. Being raised in this new American culture put a dent in the traditional gender roles and traditions my other siblings had grown up with.

Not quite a teenager, I picked up sports, such as softball, soccer, basketball, ice skating and modern dance. I also spent most of my time with my brothers who were the closest to me in age. I felt more like their little brother. They coached me in most sports, especially soccer and basketball. I felt I was always where I was supposed to be. In soccer, I was always the only girl and their little secret weapon. It was never an issue though, being the only girl, because my brothers treated me like any other player.

Sports played a very big role in who I became. Team sports gave me a sense of being part of something bigger. No matter how gifted, or not, an athlete I was, I needed to contribute to the ultimate goal, the win. What a great concept. In some situations, I had to trust a teammate whom I knew didn't have the skills, but had to trust that he or she had something to contribute to the game. In doing so, I gave that person the courage and confidence to do his or her part on the team.

Sometimes all the stars aligned and we would walk off the field with a win. Other times, not so much. I know for me though, I always came out a better player, a better teammate, a better athlete, and definitely a better overall person. Whether it was reliving the smart plays that put us on top, or examining my/our contribution to why we came up short, the defeat always came with so much more to unpack, learn and examine. Once we could get past our self-judgment, dissecting the loss was so powerful and empowering.

So liberating were my own wins, but more so my losses. The defeats were definitely a little stickier and more uncomfortable, but for me, it was in those moments – that space between the loss and the lesson – that crazy enough felt purposeful. Did I become an incredible athlete who saved all the following games after the loss? Good God no. But I always came out the other side enlightened and/or with a new perspective I never knew existed. Looking back now, it seems like I was on more losing teams than ones that won because I remember being very young and very aware of the process while I was experiencing it. Hmmmmm, that is a whole other book.

THROUGH THE EYES OF LOVE

So, did I need to go through all this pain and have to release the life I had planned for myself? Did I have to leave this relationship and create pain for the people I love so much? Could I have learned about my instincts and gifts when all was right in my world? Maybe or maybe not.

Unfortunately, we tend to learn most through contrast. I believe we are always where we are meant to be. For me, this is how my journey was laid out. My path is just that, mine.

Although I know transformation is constant, I feel very early in mine. I have a much better understanding of my own metamorphosis. One of the many gifts I have walked away with during this time is a new perspective of the man I was married to for so long. As strange as this may sound, I would not have wanted to go through this experience with anyone else but him. Inside his own pain and struggle and redefining his own life, he kept us real. Meaning, when our discussions during the separation got difficult, they were always honest, always from compassion and, most importantly, from the core of who we are, which is love. As long as we can live from the space of love, as difficult as it can be sometimes, we can trust that we will make it to the other side expanded, evolved, and better than we ever dreamed we would be.

For me, stepping into my wholeness, started in allowing my feelings to be my guide. It is as simple as this. When I felt bad, I got quiet and listened to what I needed in order to move that feeling through. If I felt good, I ran with it and did more of that. I say it is simple, but that's if – and only if – you rely on your inner faith. This means trusting that we always have the answers to every situation that we struggle with if we are willing to look and see ourselves for who we really are, with no judgment, no fear. To see, truly see, ourselves through the eyes of love. To do that, forgiveness is key. Forgiving our parents, our siblings, the bully on the bus when we were kids, the uncle who embarrassed us in front of the whole family. Most importantly, we need to find a way to forgive ourselves. Forgive ourselves for knowing better and choosing badly. For showing up when we were not supposed to or for not showing up at all. For all the self-judgment we carry. For all we have struggled to forgive ourselves for that has led us here, which is the real work needed to become whole. This is the true transformation that was already destined for me. I am more than grateful and honored to be standing strong with everyone involved, a whole woman with reverence for all the experiences that unfold in front of me.

Unlearning that we are to rely on our partners or outside sources for our joy and healing is the biggest heart-opening experience I have walked away with on my journey. I definitely see where the line can be blurred as life gets busy with bills, kids, work, and so on. It is very natural to go to something or someone outside ourselves to soothe whatever is happening within us. It is very natural. Truth is, the act of soothing does not stop there. We must take the support we get from those outside sources, because that is what it really is, and continue to soothe and heal ourselves in order to grow forward.

Grow forward, how do we do that? How do we "unbecome" what we planned for all our lives? How do we redirect our lives and continue to grow forward? Well, for me, it is one day at a time. Every day I'm aiming for any kind of small joy, waking up and being grateful for the cup of coffee I make for myself and how much I love the smell of it. Appreciating when I wake up in the morning and how beautiful my surroundings are. Ultimately, taking in every moment of being alive after the most painful experience I have ever experienced. Every moment becomes an accomplishment. Everything I do and finish is a win for me. I savor every single experience like it is my last. I now appreciate every little thing I do, see, taste, touch, read or engage in. I've begun to experience life in a way I never knew I could. All the work of meditating and listening to what was in front of me, at the moment it was in front of me, is all paying off. I am enhancing my experience in the world. I am becoming an intentional player in my own game of life and it feels amazing.

According to Washington State University's *Ask Dr. Universe*, caterpillars are born with everything they need to become butterflies. "The image of when a caterpillar enters the pupa stage and builds the sack or chrysalis, seems to me, that is when the miracle happens. It is where the caterpillar begins to turn itself into a liquid, soupy substance. Some of these parts develop over time and are visible, like the wing buds. Other parts cannot be seen. The information of these parts is stored in the caterpillar's cells, waiting to be unlocked. They are also born with the ability to make an enzyme that serves as the key to unlocking the butterfly from the chrysalis."

Just like caterpillars, we too are born with everything we need to become who we are meant to be in this world. We come into this world fully equipped with knowing what feels right and what feels wrong, no matter what we are taught. Our feelings are indicators of whether the situations we are in, suit us or not. As we grow up, we begin to live and sometimes rely only on our physical senses. We lose connection to what we were born with — the connection to ourselves. This is a relationship that is always in perfect harmony and divinely custom made for us and will never steer us in the wrong direction.

I leave you with this inspirational quote from the American poet Diane Ackerman, "I don't want to get to the end of my life and find that I lived just the length of it, I want to have lived the width of it as well." From now on, every bird I see, flower I smell and fruit I eat becomes a whole other experience. This is the life I wanted. This is the life I didn't think existed — a life that is lived with intention throughout the good and the bad. The ownership of being 100 percent responsible for creating my own path, coupled or uncoupled, is incredibly freeing and validating. Morphing in the stillness allowed me, just like the butterfly, to transform, spread my wings and fly.

ACKNOWLEDGEMENTS

I'm in constant awe of the pure wisdom of my greatest teachers, my four beautiful children, Hevyn, Harrison, Hendrix, and Hawkyns. I am forever grateful for your constant faith in me. Furthermore, the man who is always solid in who he is and loved me so much that he was able to let me go – John Pray.

ABOUT THE AUTHOR

Luz Arteaga-Pray has served the Providence, Rhode Island and Southeastern Massachusetts area for over 30 years as a licensed hairstylist. The eclectic salon environment has allowed her to work with a diverse client base including children, business professionals and artistic entrepreneurs like herself. Along the way, her occupation organically evolved into something more than just physical style. Her work blossomed into full-blown strategy sessions with her clients on how to live richer and more fulfilling lives.

As a natural motivational leader, Luz has turned those skills into another successful entrepreneurial business. Luz is now a certified Transformational Life Coach, through The Brave Thinking Institute, where she helps clients design the life they really want to live. As a leader in her local industry, Luz has mentored, taught and created outreach opportunities for her staff and salon business – leading her to become the sought-after speaker, teacher and coach she is today. *Morphing in Stillness* is her debut memoir which is also available as an audiobook. To contact the author, please visit nextlevelliving.dreambiuldercoach.com